VIA Folios 133

My Tarantella

My Tarantella

Jennifer Martelli

BORDIGHERA PRESS

Library of Congress Control Number: 2018956474

Printed in the United States.

Published by
BORDIGHERA PRESS
John D. Calandra Italian American Institute
25 West 43rd Street, 17th Floor
New York, NY 10036

VIA FOLIOS 133
ISBN 978-1-59954-130-3

CONTENTS

13	The Major Arcana of the Kitty Genovese Tarot
14	Astronomers Added the Unicorn to the Orion Constellation Family for Completeness
15	In the North End
16	In the Light of the Hanging Globe Lamp
18	A God Lives in the Amygdala
19	Discussing Elephant Puppets the Night of the Refugee Ban
20	Men Who Are Afraid of Bats
21	Stencil of Kitty Genovese on a Cinderblock Wall
22	Cervical/Turn
23	At the Border
24	Once Loosed
25	The Grape Arbor
26	Artichoke Heart
27	Kitty Genovese, Being Dead, Conflates
28	After Bird
30	The Tin Colander with Stars
32	At the Plaza de Santa Croce
33	Anniversary
35	Dear Kitty,
36	After JFK's Assassination, Things Got Really Bad
38	*Panis, Panis, Angelicus* : A Cento
39	Kim Jong-un's Half Brother was Murdered by Two Women with Poison Needles
40	Kitty Genovese is Offered a Rorschach Print Dress
41	Pomona Street
42	Gold Bug Bagatelle
43	from *Kitty Genovese: The Murder, the Bystanders, the Crime that Changed America*
44	The Passion
45	"38 Witnessed Her Death, I Witnessed Her Love: The Lonely Secret of Mary Ann Zielonko"
46	The Lavender Menace
47	Kitty Genovese Names Her Fourteen Wounds
48	Magical Thinking in the Time of Lyndon Johnson
49	My Mother's Ashtrays
50	Colonial Acres
51	Things Kitty Genovese Should Have

52 Window

53 Things that Grow Under a New Moon

54 Equinox

55 Observing Without A/Illusion

56 Necropoli

57 My Own David Bowie

58 Trump Tweets About Bloody Women

59 Eating a Hard-Boiled Egg in the Shadow of Brutalism

60 Crooked Forest

61 Genovese Basil at the Equinox

62 Winston Moseley and Kitty Genovese Talk About Transformations

63 Northern Long-Eared Bats on the Pipeline Route

64 Backstitch

66 Butoh

67 Fatal Mouths

68 I Offer Kitty Genovese Fake Fruit

Notes

Acknowledgments

About the Author

For my sisters,
Joanie and Liz

And for Catherine Susan "Kitty" Genovese
July 7, 1935 – March 13, 1964

. . . . in a society in which belief in *malocchio*—evil eye—was present at all levels . . . . the taboo is against being seen as excelling in anything, or in that close seeing which is self-knowledge. Those who go too far—Tiresias, Milton, Galileo—go blind, or like Cassandra, go unheeded.

—HELEN BAROLINI, *THE DREAM BOOK*

When the new god comes to the Big Apple, its Kyrie Eleison turns out to be a prayer Kitty Genovese simply couldn't sing.

—HARLAN ELLISON, "THE WHIMPER OF WHIPPED DOGS"

Not being a man, I bleed like this.

—BHANU KAPIL, "WHAT IS THE SHAPE OF YOUR BODY?"

THE MAJOR ARCANA
OF THE KITTY GENOVESE TAROT

1. The Giant Oaks of Kew Gardens, Queens: if leafy, indicate
    sacrifice; if bare-limbed, a refusal to look inward. To see
    through to. To throw shade.

2. The Mantis Religioso (The Praying Mantis): unusual;
    unnatural as a wire hanger, fast as a blade snapping back into
    a bone handle. Warms himself in the globe lamp hanging
    from the ceiling of the foyer in the Tudor apartments.
    Indicates ease of vanquishment.

3. The Medusa: on the field of cracked breastbone,
    gazing up at the insect, capable of suffocating Sicilian men
    with her beauty. Dangerous though beheaded. Indicates
    something will reach through half a century. But not
    moonlight nor light from the street lamp.

4. The Trinicria of Dancers' Legs: bent at the knee, toes
    pointing east, indicating sunrise in hours, begs to be plated
    in gold. Indicates the three corners of Sicily, indicates an
    insert to fit a 45 single onto a hifi so the song won't drag &
    warp. Indicates caution: go around the other corner, go the
    other way. Peril, risk.

5. The Sheaves of Wheat: gold from the loamy fields by the
    mouth of hell and Etna; sprouting from the V of the dancers'
    legs, where the blood should flow but stopped. Indicate
    infertility, indicate the time she bound her breasts to be the
    man that night she danced and danced.

6. The Queen of Mouths: thirteen mouths slit & steaming over
    her body at the equinox, lavender essence wafting up to the
    mantis, then gone, eyebrows like a crow that can find any
    heart in a field, kittenish hair shorn all spicy like desiccated
    basil, V at the nape indicating *kiss me, kiss me there.*

7. The Queen of Palms: entwined with Queen of Mouths, legs
    bent, cradling in blood and cum. Indicates friendship.
    Indicates *I hear you*, I hear you over the B-side of a Mary
    Wells single: *Boy, What Have You Done?* Indicates a gentle
    death at last. Indicates a soft palm over a body of mouths,
    covering each mouth: *I'm here, I heard you and I'm here.*

ASTRONOMERS ADDED THE UNICORN TO THE ORION CONSTELLATION FAMILY FOR COMPLETENESS

A Field Guide to the Stars and Planets

I said to my two friends, *I've been writing about Kitty Genovese because she looks like everybody I'm related to, like me with my black hair cut short into a pixie.* We stood on the cobblestone sidewalk off Hanover Street, outside the store that sold Italian horns, Christ heads, Befana witches, hollow sugared eggs with scenes of the Passion where the yolk once was, rabbits' feet dyed pink.

A big man in a weight-lifting belt tried to pass around us. He was walking two dogs: a roan pit bull and a toy terrier. In a falsetto voice, I said to the dogs, *Hi babies! Hey baby,* the man said back. I asked my friends, *How do you pronounce her name?* Olivia said, *Well, we'd say Gen-Oh-Vay-Zee.* Laurette said, *Maybe you're writing about her because she wasn't heard, or she was heard and not listened to.*

I was about to tell them that Kitty's brother said their name like the crime family, *Gen-Oh-Veez,* because some Italians didn't want people to hear that long vowel at the end. But Olivia said, *We're unicorns, you know, Italian women who write, we're that rare.* I wanted espresso with a lemon rind and rock candy anyway. At the cafe, we admired each other's boots: one of us wore boots with stacked heels, one pair fringed, my boots came up over my knees. All black, tucked under our iron chairs.

IN THE NORTH END

Boston loomed, lit: a wasp's nest ignited and inhaled. My friend's
lungs stopped for five sweet panic-seconds. Two millennia ago,
Sappho said *in some future time someone will think of you.* I said *count.*
In nineteen-nineteen, the brick streets in the North End flooded
with a million gallons of thick blackstrap molasses. My friend's big
red heart beat: four valves vibrating, a mandolin tremolo. *Count.* The
asters. The Pleiades.

IN THE LIGHT OF THE HANGING GLOBE LAMP

Maybe there were 37 witnesses. Maybe 38.
Maybe there were 2.

Maybe someone fell asleep in front of the television set.
Maybe the gold-painted metal TV tray still held a plate or an ashtray
    or a Manhattan.
Maybe someone dozed watching "Petticoat Junction" or "Death Valley
    Days,"
and the drone of static after the National Anthem after the test pattern,
    that maybe
looked like crosshairs
was white noise in a dream about snow.

Maybe Winston Moseley drove around for an hour.
Maybe because he knew she was a lesbian.
Maybe because she was woman and *they were easier and didn't fight back.*

Maybe she was stabbed 13 times. No, 14.
Maybe the one through the lung made it harder to scream.
Maybe the one through the throat whistled air.
Maybe the stab wounds looked like whispering lips.

Maybe it sounded like a man and woman fighting outside a bar.
Maybe the neighbor (who sold her the poodle
to give to Mary Ann after a lovers' spat)
was too afraid, was too drunk.

Maybe Winston Moseley's eyes after he raped her
in the vestibule of the Tudor Apartments and snapped
his knife back into its pearl handle.

Maybe the knife didn't have a pearl handle.
Maybe there are so many different pet names
for Catherine: Kitty, Kay, Cathy, Chicky, Rina.

Maybe, because that night in March just before the equinox
he raped her like a praying mantis
backwards,
and doing it after she was nearly dead.
Or maybe like a *preying* mantis, his skinny limbs bent.

Over Kitty's prone and crooked body.

That way.

A GOD LIVES IN THE AMYGDALA

I heard Amy Winehouse today, jacked up fast & techno, for my heart.
The leaves fell the way Rilke saw them fall: all motioning *no, no, no.*

I heard the brown bats that roost under the bridge over the lead mills.
And the cats crying in heat with the warn & want of a baby.

I live in a jewel-toned neighborhood. One day, as I strolled past the
        quietest house,
a small forest of Queen of Night tulips
blossomed into a whole night sky.

Next day, each Queen's stamen weakened, let loose & wept.

Do you know that nothing outside of our mouths will save us?
A god lives in the amygdala, but he is weak, too, asleep under the new
        moon.
Did you see an angel's viscera across the sky?

Back when I was young and always broken hearted, I, too, fell into a
        fever and drank
vodka chilled next to fat halved lemons in the bowl.

DISCUSSING ELEPHANT PUPPETS THE NIGHT OF THE REFUGEE BAN

Elephant puppets so big ten men can fit under their pipe bodies
and manipulate four fat limbs and a trunk: gray veils mimicking a
      pachydermic funeral

and lapis lazuli eyes, big as a bruise on a thigh.

We talk about them over an olive sampler at Mia Casa—
little bistro tucked into the clapboard block between a bar and a bar—

cobblestones, leaded windows, paned—

there's that uncanny dip, that sweet valley of something that looks
like something else: deep eyes, big as the loaf on the plate, big as a hole

in the middle of a nation.

This is not my house.
We talk about the mammoth elephant puppets,

how they seem to dance but it's men
running under the articulated pipes and the sheer veils.

MEN WHO ARE AFRAID OF BATS

. . . . it kills me when I think about it. The black leather gloves
and all cuts, all through the gloves
on both her hands . . . .
—Sophia Farrar

D.H. Lawrence described the bats
in Pisa, Italy,
as *serrated wings against the sky,*

like a glove,

a black glove thrown up at the light . . . .

He called the flight of bats
Dark air life looping and confused them
for a flight of swallows

in the Italian dusk. He feared them, too,
those *old rags.* Sophia

yelled to the neighbor peeking through the slit
in his apartment door for a towel, *Karl, please,*

for the blood
the torn open cuts.

Kitty was my friend
and I knew she was hurt

Sophia said

that was my reason for flying . . . .

STENCIL OF KITTY GENOVESE ON A CINDERBLOCK WALL

My friend found it first. Does it matter that we have the same name? Neither of us was looking for her; nevertheless, Kitty Genovese's face appeared one day on that old wall that no one lived or worked behind anymore: the grunge garage, bankrupted, down the street, off the square where it floods all the time from the rains and the rivers that flow deep beneath the ground. *There's something wrong with that area,* she said, *I don't like my kids walking there.* But she walked there that day and took the photo on her phone of Kitty stenciled on the wall, and asked me, *Is this Kitty? Is this who you're writing about?* She was barely formed, barely filled in, except for the contours of her face: the messy bob, the arched brow, oh that beautiful top lip curved. Someone must have projected her from a Kodak carousel, from a single beam shining through a vintage slide. Did I tell you my friend and I have the same name? That I'd been thinking of Kitty for most of the summer? That we were both haunted?

CERVICAL/TURN

I searched the internet for an Italian

sonnet, found: two round stones
tied with string, a tintype of an old

master wearing a crown of twisted linden
leaves, a pre-historic painting

from a cave deep within Avellino
of a fat dusty umber owl

its head in full rotation—

Yeah, so, I'm looking for the cervical
turn, the way to the way back,
a volta protected by

fourteen vertebrae. My quarrel
is this ancient blood within myself. Black
linden leaves reflecting a million eyes.

AT THE BORDER

Just my knee bent on the avocado couch in the old Kodak photo.
I wore orange fishnet tights with tonal opaques underneath to
contrast

textures. Even at seven, I knew about layering. My hand, cropped off
mid-
reach to my baby sister, was tanned, burnt umber up to my wrist,

and then just the photo's white border, with the date: May, 69.
I would brown up fast like everybody on my father's Italian side.
Brown

by Easter through Halloween. Once, a new neighbor asked my father
what race is she? and my father never spoke to her
again.

ONCE LOOSED

Pulled my mother's stockings (runs stanched with clear polish)
from her tangled drawer, pulled one leg

down over my head, pulled the toe up
and I had the snout of a pig. The platinum blonde

gibbous moon shone through the window, over the bush
with white paper buds. The moon sang

I Will Follow Him. An old scapular lay coiled in the drawer:
Santa Maria Goretti or Kitty Genovese, their images on soft wool, roses

spilling from their stab wounds, eyes like black olives. I couldn't see
or speak well with that torn mesh over my face. My hair,

once loosed,
was electric, attracted to the metal edges of my house.

THE GRAPE ARBOR

in Mr. Ternullo's yard was a tangled mess of black vines, the few leaves
        glowing
under moonlight. I've stayed up too late watching scary movies like

I did with my mother, eating blue cheese and Saltines, my feet tucked
        under her thighs
for warmth on the couch. In the movie tonight, a girl who died a
        violent death crawls

out of an old TV, a vat of oil, a sliver of broken mirror. Her black hair
crowns first, then her eyes, and then she looks for you. Mr. Ternullo
        kept big glass

jugs of wine so purple it felt like a bruise. His wine hurt
deep inside parts of the body, could dye bones, burn your heart.
        Sometimes it felt

like your lungs deflated, the booze so strong. He had shelves of wine jugs
in his cool cellar: rows and rows of glossy black light. All my fears

have come to pass: nothing could ever quell them.

ARTICHOKE HEART

And another of my mother's lies was the prize
dug from the heart of the artichoke.

And the heart of the artichoke was a dilated cervix.
And the dilated cervix was a single choke-fringed eye.

The eye was the stigma
of the plant protected by thorny leaves and stamen.

I scraped the meaty pith
at the torn-off tips with my milk teeth.

She told me to dip the meat of the leaves in butter: warm, silken.
She said *eat all the way to the inside:* there was a prize.

But it was soft, the heart, and I imagined
a small plastic baby doll, tiny as my own girl thumb

lying unclothed
on the blue-green velvet.

KITTY GENOVESE, BEING DEAD, CONFLATES

Blind bats circle the phone wires, echolocate.
The night is a night

of a new moon: deepest blue, God's favorite Bakelite bowling ball.
Late winter thunder. The bats

aren't bats at all, they are my leather hands, black-gloved
over my eyes. The sky expands on the rutted grooves

of my Phil Ochs folk album, the one with a ballad about me. The metal
tip of my tongue drags across the surface, like a scream. Love

brings me back to you. What is it that you want?
My love is deep blue almost as dark as my hair. My love skips

in a scrape, lodges in a rut. My love circles and circles like the bats
around the grape arbors. My love loves reflection, my own face

surfacing on the black ice scrim. I peek through
the sliced webbing of my gloves, forget to protect

my belly and throat. Golden birds, velvet bats
escape my mouth and no one hears me.

AFTER BIRD

I.

In the kitchen with the pink oven, my mother roasted beef each
        Sunday, and we had a choice
of brown gravy or the blood. On the stove (with buttons that heated
        the coils until they glowed,

uterine snakes) she'd simmer bracciola: meat tied in string. We'd
        sop
bone broth with salad and bread. Sometimes, we'd eat on black metal
        TV trays,

all matte painted with fat gold roses.

II.

I had a blue plastic kitty bank:
she had long black lashes and arched brows
and she was molded sitting
on her hind legs with a slit cut
in the back of her neck
to slip the coins in.

I had a doll with hair
coiled inside her hollow
body: you could pull the hank
from her crown. I had a doll
with the head of a pure white dog
and the body of a woman—no,
a girl: flat-chested.

III.

I had white fringe go-go boots and I'd dance when my uncle came
        over. I'd dance
to Nancy Sinatra: on the gold-flecked linoleum, on the flagstones out
front littered with white andromeda buds, out by the hibachi on the
        kidney-shaped patio.

Paper lanterns and beaked masks hung from the willow tree to
    the clothesline.

IV.

I had a grandma who came downstairs for leftovers. Once, she talked
    about how
sweet and dense Hanover Street smelled, long after they'd cleaned the
    molasses
that flooded the North End in a tide of the cheapest brown sugar.
For years in the heat, it smelled of hermits and gingerbread men.

V.

Inevitably, it was my mother who rose from the golden flowers painted
on the old TV trays (long since rusted in the cellar). She was unhealed
even in death, still confused. She came out of the rose's mouth like an
afterbirth. That night, the sky was as thin as a giant vat of molasses, so
it was easy to come through, to split the seams.

VI.

My mother said after her own mother died, she saw her rocking in a
    chair on their front porch.

My mother poured herself over me, sweet and sticky, into my mouth

and my eyes were stuck shut by the lashes. I had an image of my mother

inside my eyes: an afterbird.

VII.

We had an electric opener with a magnet to hold the can
while it turned against the blade.
Saturdays: we ate from a tin.

THE TIN COLANDER WITH STARS

Which eye should David Bowie peek through the crack in the kitchen
        door
to see you with? The right one, blue and tight, the good girl?

Or the one that can't close its black: an eclipse
in the middle of the day, a cervix? Shiny button on a neo-white shirt?

The red lipstick over your open mouth, did you smear it
with the back of your hand? Will Bowie see you peel down your jeans?

His lightning bolt—where will it land? Across your face
all electric blue, all red from your lethal temple zig-zagging the
        eyelid, the mouth?

All day I've thought of stars: me, unbalanced, cored and loosed from
        the tin
colander-colored sky, dogged diamonds squeezed 1,000 years in a fist.

I search the junk drawer for my mezzaluna to rock against the oak
        board—
the old one, shaped into a pig with my grandpa's saw. His old belts
        used for straps.

They hung on their hooks, brown snakes, *you'll get the strap:* they
        hung in the hall
next to the wine bottles in wicker baskets, next to the herbs, near cool
        stone.

The runes you throw portend Bowie, with his one working eye and
        his bolt.
Did you feel the tremors? All along the earth's fault-line seams? Did
        you hoard candles?

What is perishable in the pantry? What will keep in the autumn heat?
Hot pasta water pours through the holes punched in my old
        colander—

dented thing, dropped or flung, I stole it from my mother. Across its
 convex concavity,
stars and stars and stars punched through with a nail from the workshop.

Will Bowie be healed now that he's dead? I'm owed the past year, I'm
 owed 50: bad eye
anisocoric: can't constrict, can't whistle or kiss, won't change color, be
 blue.

AT THE PLAZA DE SANTA CROCE

most pigeons' wings shone deep
indigo against the basilica's terra cotta facade.

Before I could enter the cathedral, I had to buy a blue
paper shawl to cover my bare shoulders:

my left blade with its one-ink tattoo of a bass clef, the right,
the dark still face of Kitty Genovese.

The lady said to save the shawl for all the churches in Italy.
For one euro, I was winged and God wasn't offended.

ANNIVERSARY

A mouth just bloodied.
—Sylvia Plath, "Poppies in July"

1.

A year ago this summer, I grew
Genovese basil in a fake clay pot I'd move around my home to follow

the arc of direct sunlight. I've thought of Kitty Genovese for a long
      time: her mouth.
How easy it is to open a mouth

anywhere, to split it & split it. I can't love what I don't fear.

2.

For my "Plath's 'Poppies in July' Party," I bought fake rubies shaped
      like pears,
wore a red skirt, hung lanterns

from the maples in my backyard. The skirt=a poppy,
the lanterns=love, the pear-shape=eyes or a womb. The rubies?

The first time I was slapped in the mouth.

3.

A year ago this summer, I saw
a man wearing a silk-screen t-shirt: *Trump that bitch.*

Hillary's mouth was a red slash.
I saw a woman wearing a silk-screen t-shirt: *Trump that bitch.* So I
      knew it was over.

After the solstice or before the equinox.

4.

I thought of Kitty so hard, I was afraid she would manifest, smiling—
in the dark corner of my laundry room, from my closet hook where
      belts hang—

I thought of her so deeply, it was like sex, far up & slow &
violent. And then I became unafraid.

I knew she was gone.

5.

This is how the Queen of Night tulips toppled: first, their lips
let loose the dark petals:

they puddled like a silk gown. Then from the dug-up dirt,
grow four rock cairns, high as my knee: beach stones gray

with white veins stacked.

6.

I still can't love what I don't fear.
Even though I'm throwing a party, we all know

there's sadness underneath the flagstones.
It's a farewell party. We'll leave claw & bite marks.

In the future, someone might know what we meant.

DEAR KITTY,

I am breaking my own rule talking to the dead for the sake of
the living. I want to imply a sense of intimacy between us. I want
witnesses and eavesdroppers. I don't believe in consciousness after
death. I believe you are gone. But I found a Kodak of me in front
of my aluminum Christmas tree the Advent after you died: my hair,
short and black like yours in the mug shot, and my cousin in her
pink Danskin had your dark bow and arrow eyebrows. The silver was
meant to look like a frozen fir tree, the needles iced and shining under
the moon. Did the sky above Kew Gardens open like a peacock's tail,
all dim oculi, shadow-eyed? Windows are dangerous: we locked every
one, the aunts, my sisters and all the cousins the night Albert DeSalvo
escaped. What is it about us Italians? We fear birds and we fear eyes,
but mostly we whisper. Even your killer's son feared the vowel at the
end of your name. Your stab wounds were lips, they were eyes too.
Did you know Mary Ann waited upstairs in your bed? Did you know
Sophia held you in the foyer on the slick tiles? Did you know your
mother had a stroke after you died? Your story is the *Bossa Nova*. It is
Downtown. Your hair was brown black. Women loved you. It hurts
my hoarse throat, my blue heart.

AFTER JFK'S ASSASSINATION, THINGS GOT REALLY BAD

Why are you writing about her?

Kitty puts things in order, things I thought I'd forgotten:
all the earth tones. I try to describe the color of blood: copper and
baked red, my front steps, bricks, terra cotta. Kitty Genovese was
menstruating that night, the Kotex was held in place with the
    garter straps,
how my mother showed me. It was in his way but

How does Kitty order things?

she was not his first. He burnt the first woman: lit a chiffon scarf
    on fire and
stuck it up *there* inside of her. He made sure he burnt her *there*.
    No one
knew who did this to poor Annie Mae Johnson because she
    was black
and Kitty was white. He burnt the first woman before she was
    even dead. My mother

Do you miss your mother? What she told you?

said she would lose her mind if my sisters or I died
before she did, told me never to talk that way but I feared she
would die before me. I feared it and she did. She had
a turban: sheer ecru that only showed her black widow's peak
she wore to be dressy and when she'd come home it smelled like
menthol Trues. Kitty's mother's heart was broken. She couldn't
walk down the aisle in the church past the people in the wooden
pews. She wasn't told about her daughter's deflated lungs or
    how he
flung the Kotex to the corner of the vestibule. She wouldn't
    ever go
back to Queens not even for the '64 World's Fair. But I feel
    like I

How does Kitty order things?

>   remember the big TVs in Almy's Department Store, two whole
>   aisles of
>   RCAs built into wooden consoles, antennae like antlers and
>   everybody was silent or crying. One woman said *we're glued*
>   *here, we're*
>   *glued to the TV.* They said they killed the President because he
>   was
>   Catholic. My mother held my hand. I didn't know what
>   that meant. I was
>
>   afraid; my mother was crying. We went home. She made me
>   sit on the
>   terra cotta front steps of our new ranch home. She gave me
>   something sweet and cold. My mother

Why are you writing about her?

>   looked beautiful in her chiffon turban.
>   She had a tin ashtray from the '64 World's Fair in Queens.
>
>   I saw a burnt out building with Kitty's face
>   spray painted on the old baked brick. Block words
>   circled her like a halo: *what is true? who will tell?*

PANIS, PANIS, ANGELICUS : A CENTO

I love you because I am Italian and you wear it better.
I am afraid I shall not know an American with a familiar kind of face.

I'll brew my wine from gold to gray,
my nipple like the nib of a pen.

Your flesh was unused tissue:
they say you lurk here still, perhaps.

I got lonely because I was going extinct
from giving and giving and giving.

There was a smell of woman made spring there—
narrow windows on a narrow alley,

only the evil eyes of a thousand buildings
that nothing, nothing can shatter.

The heat sits on my body with the cumulative weight of dream men:
He is creeping prick first/into my sleeping bag cunt.

(We wish to dam this female tide:
Something would have to break through with a life of its own.)

KIM JONG-UN'S HALF BROTHER WAS MURDERED BY TWO WOMEN WITH POISON NEEDLES

They licked the needles with their tongues after they'd dished dirt
    about his mother.
They licked the needles after they spoke of their own sopped-up blood.

They pushed the needles in and out in and out of a tight salt-filled
    strawberry.
Needles honed sharp enough to pierce his coat, sharp as the tack
    my mother stepped on: clean through her left heel callus.

I saw it happen. I was lying on the floor looking up her skirt to see
    where I came from.
I saw it happen and felt bad because I'd left the tack on the shag rug,
    the pointed end hidden in a jungle of golden fibers.
She told me not to look there ever again, not to look ever, *ever*.

Two women with poison needles made their point. One wrapped
    lamb's wool
around her anklets so the bells wouldn't give her away.

KITTY GENOVESE IS OFFERED A RORSCHACH PRINT DRESS

When I had cut it enough, it didn't look like a woman anymore.
Walter Kovacs, "The Watchmen"

A pony-skin
shift; black spots on white

faux leather. Go-go
boots. Skin

will move on you,
yes, all monochrome slick

slippery when you get to be
the girl in the night club

where they make
dildos from crutch pads. Black

matches your eyes,
your hair. When you dance

animals will run down
that dress. Shadows

of clouds rushing across your flat
torso. Animals. Leslie Gore

singing, *You don't*
own me. White

below your eyes, white
will cup & cradle your black.

POMONA STREET

My bunny-fur earmuffs were pearl gray
and maybe faux; they shone against my black
cat hair. I wore them around my neck
to hide my nape with its little V.
At Pia's beauty salon
in her cellar with the beehived
women listening to Petula Clark
I begged not to have it shorn into a pixie.
After, to stop my crying, Quinn the bookie
gave me something sweet on a stick.
I asked for green but got red. I asked
for my mother, but got my aunt.

GOLD BUG BAGATELLE

When I learned to spell penis, I cut
two dolls from math paper, kept the girl, gave the boy

to my best friend in second grade, Lorraine, who wore kilts
with real pins and that made me love her. We had

the idea of penis, rubbed the floppy flat
couple against each other. The silverfish and moths

were all over the classroom that warm fall, pressed
between pages of books, falling from the window shades.

Our teacher's hair was bleached white, but her brows
were dark. She wore a pin on her green wool

suit: a small frog encrusted with crystals to look like garnets
and emeralds. Her charm bracelet had gold bugs

dangling: three species of beetles, grasshopper, an embossed
lady bug, hornet, a praying mantis. When she motioned me

up to her desk, the bugs on her wrist played a sweet
high bagatelle.

FROM *KITTY GENOVESE: THE MURDER, THE BYSTANDERS, THE CRIME THAT CHANGED AMERICA*

Gold Bug,

    soft enough

                  part-
ner who   wore

      fedoras.

  At

the Village, downtown

      Kitty felt free   a
sexual being,   a green hornet

      around the dance floor

.

    The

      infectious

ladies

           dance

   and leave,
    wave

THE PASSION

In the basement of St. Nicholas's Orthodox Church
on Bridge Street Neck in Salem

I hugged my friend who wore, on her herringbone coat's lapel,
three gold pins: a dragonfly, a bee, a beetle

with a pearl thorax. I said I'd always wanted a gold bug
pin, and she said, *choose one, but not the dragonfly,*

which is what I hoped she'd say. I chose
the beetle, but I have to tell you how

the fourteen stations of the cross—each panel
marking the hours of a gruesome death—were embellished

in gold leaf, so that the metal absorbed the dim lights
and shone. The haloes, the icons, the women weeping,

the crown of leafy thorns, even the strips of skin torn
from the lash, the stab wound through ribs, shone.

"38 WITNESSED HER DEATH, I WITNESSED HER LOVE: THE LONELY SECRET OF MARY ANN ZIELONKO"

—LuLu LoLo's play about Kitty Genovese

In between character monologues, women danced and bent, each split//
deeper, a grind, a lower plié. One dancer performed butoh, crawled//
across the floor, pulled a stick of white chalk out of her mouth//tapped
the stick on the stage at the Robert Moses Theater, outlined her own
body and then played dead.//Here's who knew the secret: Karl, who
watched Kitty raped at the bottom of his stairs,//the gamblers at Ev's
Eleventh Hour Bar, the neighbor boy who took Kitty's old hand-me-
down blue jeans, neighbors who saw//Mary Ann's light-colored eyes
dilate when Kitty came home, oh maybe Kitty's parents, though//
they buried her in a white dress like for //First Holy Communion or a
wedding, and they took//the couple's dog from the Tudor Apartment in
Kew Gardens. They left the pop-a-bead//necklace, the hot plate, they
left the leather wallets Kitty and Mary Ann exchanged//for Christmas.
They left a flannel shirt. The folk albums.

THE LAVENDER MENACE

Kitty practices typing on the Olivetti Lettera-22.
The smoke from her menthol True makes her squint.
The type bars swing like the Rockette's silver-tight kickline.
Her Bauhaus desk is teak and dark, hardest wood you can find.

A quick brown fox jumps over a lazy dog.
But wouldn't she rather be precise?
The quick brown fox jumps over the lazy dog.

Now is the time for all good men to come to the aid of their country.
Now is the time for all good men to come to the aid of their party.

The ribbon is black on top, and below, red.

Like the sky at night without a moon and the sidewalk
outside her apartment, below.

Her typewriter has a pale purple clamshell case, with clasps.

When she pulls it from under her bed, totes it down the hall,
her sweet girlfriend tells her she looks like a Pan Am stewardess

rushing off to an eleventh hour flight.

KITTY GENOVESE NAMES HER FOURTEEN WOUNDS

The first shouldered the new-moon sky.

The second was a single blue oculus on the tail of a fearful peacock.

Here was the last wound that could have saved me.

There's the mouth below the mouth across my throat.

Three wounds killed the dark brown bats flitting around my face.

And that wound down there let out the baby I would never have.

A bouquet of asters. And still: who knows which was the fatal one? So
        many wounds like the ice slivers in that first amber
        Manhattan
                breaking sobriety.

Another eye, a human one, no, two eyes staring up at the globe lamp,
        looking for God.

And another mouth opened up, tried to cry for my mother, like
        in that nightmare of not being able to run.

Labia majora, those swollen lips wet with (menstrual) blood.

The next-to-last almost swallowed up a praying mantis.

The very last wound: the palm of woman calling kitty, kitty, kitty,
        kitty, kitty, kitty.

MAGICAL THINKING IN THE TIME OF LYNDON JOHNSON

Don't walk in spike heels in the Village: your ankle bones will hit high
    notes.

Don't dye your black hair that color red: you'll bleed soon.

Don't wash your white blouse with bleach: it will yellow, grow curled
    fingernails.

Don't throw away your opaque tights; stanch the run with clear nail
    polish.

Years later, Petula Clark sang *don't sleep in the subway, darlin', don't
    stand in the pouring rain.*

Don't think your mother's widow's peak won't attract crows.

Don't forget the V of hair at the nape of your neck. Don't forget it
    when your hair grows out.

Don't forget to eat Jell-O mold salad so your nails will grow tough
    as horses' hooves.

Don't forget to leave your living room window open all night: you'll
    hear the spring thaw and freeze thaw and freeze thaw and
    freeze.

Don't forget. Don't forget.

MY MOTHER'S ASHTRAYS

She had a chunky amber glass one,

cleaned-out clamshell, and a tin ashtray from the '64 World's Fair
with grooves I could rub my finger on back and forth,

lick off the tar.

My mother burnt a hole in Aunt Agnes's gray wool suit,
right in the arm while they were driving. *Dope* my aunt said.
She hated our Italian hair. My mother could slick down smooth

my pixie on picture day, squinting, a cigarette in her lips.
My mother spritzed me with Jean Naté
from the yellow bottle before I left for school.

I found the picture: how I stared at the photographer,
my chin high over the Peter Pan collar, my little brown

eyes mug shot steady.

COLONIAL ACRES

Up from the beach and near the clay farms
where the Mulligans raised pigs,

Mr. Festa built rows of ranch houses with pink or
burnt sienna kitchens and named three streets

after his kids—Anne and Johnny and Joey—named
one after his wife Camille, one for his mother Assunta,

and called this Colonial Acres in gothic font. Some homes
had Pilgrim touches: lanterns with electric flames

on the front porches, gold eagles on the flag poles,
eagles spread eagle above the doors. Noe, Simonini,

Ternullo, DeMarco, Cardinale
(who was shot execution-style), DeNitto, Caporale,

Grenga, Magnifico, Ceci (whose mother was a witch),
Salamone, Stagno, Polito, Gravalese (who ground pork

and sage into translucent gut tubes with a steel crank
grinder on the flagstone patio). The leaves on the grape arbors

were olive-green-black and at night steam
rose from the gardens and there were bones.

THINGS KITTY GENOVESE SHOULD HAVE

Three scoop-neck Danskins: black, forest green, garnet.
Matchbook from The Swing Rendevous on MacDougal Street.
Pearl choker necklace (which rests on the nape of her neck)
and a plunging V-back baby blue sateen fitted dress.
A horse-hair brush and a brown bone comb.
Ink sketch of Kitty looking out an apartment window in Kew Gardens.
Also by Mary Ann Zielonko: oil painting of the sketch, cubist,
         burnt colors.
Black flats with jeweled clips (smoky diamond). Pumps.
Cigarette pants. Tin espresso pot. Mascara.
A fedora for when she's the man. Piaf.
Petula Clark's *Downtown*.
And *Ces bottes sont faites pour marcher* had she lived.
Full moon. Five minutes. Window. Window.

WINDOW

Once, during a long warm August dusk, I heard a bat outside my
    bedroom window.
I stopped shaking my sheets out, stood by the sheer white curtains
    covering my window.

I decorated my backyard with black and red paper lanterns hanging
    from the maples.
I strung five lengths of small white globe lights along my patio, below
    my window.

Owls' feathers aren't as heavy as the wings of a bat: those leathered
    long finger bones.
My black cat stays inside: she watches things fly, watches mammals
    from her window.

My neighbor put a full-length cracked mirror on the sidewalk for
    trash or for free.
I was too ashamed to take it and pick out glass slivers, so I watched,
    crouched by my window.

When I put my cat down, she was as still as onyx, cold as Pluto's
    moon, useless as God.
All the paper lanterns in my backyard were eaten-through masks, eye
    holes like windows.

I have a small china bowl, with a tiny brown owl on its lip; the owl
    looks down into painted blue stars.
I keep my name in gold on a chain cupped safe in that bowl on the
    sill under my window.

THINGS THAT GROW UNDER A NEW MOON

1. Rust on the mezzaluna

2. dreams of a woman sleeping

3. moisture on the great oaks' leaves

4. gray cat's green eyes

5. the pool of streetlamp light around the lip-red Fiat

6. pool of black ice melted

7. pool of blood on the hot top

8. fourteen wounds

9. his irises

10. her irises

11. and her irises in a dream beneath sky blue eyelids

12. her aureole

13. not the heart, not anybody's heart

14. the length of a window shade

15. a myth

16. Ursa Major

17. the tear in the middle of equinox, throwing off delicate balance

18. the shadow over the moon caused by the world.

EQUINOX

Time clutched its toad-green watering can and dowsed the soil
to grow things to kill. Time hummed that old diamond-back song,
    hummed

the song of cigarettes.

Time watered, and dawn seeped up from the ground
well before the hot sun rose hungry, ready to singe

the tender shoots. Time poured more drink
and a hunting knife grew, reflecting light. Then a lung,

then a heart, seven layers of skin.

Time gave water to a small patch and Sappho rose. Then the Pleiades,

soft and white as asters, not yet
planted. Then Sappho's lover under the grape arbor, entwined in lattice.

Time will kill her, too.

Time brushed its hands on daisy-embroidered overalls. Time thought,
I should plant round things: vinyl albums, snakes

eating their own tails, belly buttons, cancer cells, dilation (eye & cervical),
street lamp globes, new moons, penumbras, small circles of friends.

Time drew on the yellow papyrus, just poking through, *I should grow*

a dark-haired girl who is afraid of all of this. I should grow
her wounds and purple scars.

OBSERVING WITHOUT A/ILLUSION

The patch of garden in front of the apartment has a bed of smooth
    stones: gray
on a gray scale, gray on pearl.

The black petals almost all fallen from the garden of Queen of Night
tulips: black stigmas bobbing on their long stems.

The Department of Family & Child Services diagonal: the facade
    clean white
stucco, picture windows, and vertical blinds, some bent.

Beyond and behind, a cell tower perpendicular to the sky, a spire.

NECROPOLI

I drive home up the arm bone of Cape Cod
and the Sagamore Bridge rises

before me: a humped moon, unlit.

What do you say to someone whose cancer comes back?
I mean, after complimenting his good looks. We had agreed

not to utter the word "President" for four years. And we spoke

of Queens, how expensive even the outer boroughs have become. I
        talked about
the shape of Cape Cod, how it points back at the rest of us

in Massachusetts. I've always distrusted

the red bogs down here. Over dinner, we discussed the stone circles
        the Celts
left all over Britain and France: were they calendars

or temples, necropoli? Were they infrastructure projects, endless
construction? Wood then stone then sunlight then moonlight.

What's changed when the solstice angle returns to light the slaughter
        stone—
Who would be alive. Would we still be angry.

MY OWN DAVID BOWIE

During the Bicentennial, when the Tall Ships
sailed into the Harbor, I wore a tube top
with red and white stripes like the flag's
bloody wounds. I wore sailor pants deep navy blue
with two rows of white buttons tracing the shape
of my uterus. I wasn't smiling: I leaned against the rail at the pier
away from my family and dangled over Boston.

I thought my heart must be a place to worship
because it was serious and heavy, gold-veined
as the Italian marble quarried for a church. I wouldn't even have
a Walkman until '79, but I could feel my own
David Bowie. Didn't I love the line: *Ain't there a woman
I can sock on the jaw?* I sang it wrong from the start: *they pulled in
just behind the fridge, he lays her down.*

But something is always something else:
A loaf of bread is a stone. A fish is a snake.
God (is a father who hates my bare shoulders) can show mercy, or not.
My tube top was a bandage, was a hostage's blindfold, a country.
My sailor buttons were tender & etched with anchors, stars
in a mid-spring constellation.

TRUMP TWEETS ABOUT BLOODY WOMEN

At the gelateria on *Via Fausto Dionisi*,

a British couple read their Twitter feeds out loud.

I consider passing for Canadian.

I wish I spoke Italian, but that tongue

was long ago nailed to the wood paneling

by a great-great-grandparent

next to the pepper in the second kitchen

downstairs, where I wasn't listening.

There was a sadness to the language, all gun-

metal, pulled from the sulfur mines deep

within the heart of that old country, but

who am I to guess what it meant?

They were so proud to be rid of the tongue

that jutted out of Medusa's head and broke

legs. Here in Italy, I can't pass—not even with

my black eyes, my hair, not with my olive skin.

EATING A HARD-BOILED EGG IN THE SHADOW OF BRUTALISM

It's always been a love/hate thing: the raw

concrete of Boston City Hall, conceived the same year

as I. The walls refuse the ivy & the vine

& the windows repeat over & over in rows. The face

refuses to be pretty, to be light. It shows its bones. The devil

listens for show-offs, for pride. My parents never called me

beautiful, *facia brute*, they'd say: ugly face

to keep me safe from jealous hexes. The egg with its green skin

over a yolk cooked hard to a gray ball, & salted

with the small packets I pocketed from the coffee shop

on the other side of City Hall Plaza, splits easily. The yolk

like the sun in partial eclipse. The mayor dropped a large

gold coin as he ran across the Plaza, his lucky coin.

It bounced on the ground & rolled & rolled till it fell

on its side near the mouth of the Blue Line where I sat

with my egg. It landed, sober pyramid to the sky. Soon

a lunar shadow will cross the whole country, right through

its heartland. Most architects deny the movement called

brutalism. In seven years, the totality of the eclipse

will cover my state. From the Common behind me,

I can hear the sirens, the horns & clapping, the chants.

CROOKED FOREST

Cusp of spring is the best time to see the bent
fir trees in that secret grove

deep inside Europe: fifty-foot trunks shorn after the snows and so
scoliotic, they drag their witch bellies

across the forest floor. Today, I trolled

the president of my country. *You are not well,*
I typed. *If you could feel shame, then shame*

on you. After a long time in winter,
the brook behind my house muddies, low

and thawing. Sweet lavender peeks through
my house's cracked foundation.

GENOVESE BASIL AT THE EQUINOX

A late summer bee comes to drink the spicy nectar, cares nothing for
    the desiccated herb,
only its blue flowers. I fill a brown bag

with humped leaves for pesto. Once I've shorn the plant
the basil will be gone, but the seeds have dispersed: I can grow

pots of basil all year in a window facing south. I think,
    too, of a haircut
a dark pixie with bangs.

The sweet green oil, slick.
The aroma floats
    on the air like a cry.

WINSTON MOSELEY AND KITTY GENOVESE TALK ABOUT TRANSFORMATIONS

~~That night, your Fiat, all Italian and red, glowed~~
~~even with no moon, shone like your lips.~~

> That night, all the windows, blinds pulled down like eyelids
> over rapid eye movement on the other side, watching a dream.

~~Your screams: soft fruit, maybe golden brown pears, falling from the~~
~~trees.~~

> Your knife: the only part of you that was hard.

~~I never hated you, never, not even your skin. I never loved you.~~

> I never loved you, even in my death. Me, all eyeshadowed
> with fourteen mouths.

~~Me, into a crouching loci.~~

> Me, into a ghost.

NORTHERN LONG-EARED BATS ON THE PIPELINE ROUTE

Piled like odd left-hand gloves, the bats

sleep high in their caves on the boreal line: above the waxy

junipers, the yew trees, the pines. Their suede ears,

a million times more subtle than ours, pick up the soft

stirring of the snakes knotted deep down in their hibernaculum

thawing, well past St. Brigid's Day. In their bat-dreams,

the snakes' hisses become a stream of gold milk from a warm teat,

tear of a defensive wound, a long slow leak serrating the air.

BACKSTITCH

When I think about the people who woke
at three in the morning

hearing a woman scream
and turned away

from their windows, turned
back in bed, because

they thought they heard
not a murder but

a lovers' spat,
that is,

if the man knows you, he can
hurt you, and

when I think of the scant

number of words in the police report
of the rape and murder of that black

woman just weeks
before this white

woman, how they
had to loop like a sewing stitch

moving backwards

from Kitty Genovese's murder
to Annie Mae Robinson's, when I think

of how he used rape
as a weapon, the burning silk

scarf shoved inside her, the hunting blade
stopped only by pubic bone, when

I think of the chance
the just-maybe-chance

that maybe
some witnesses knew, could sense

Kitty loved

differently, that
she didn't date boys

and so their hands hovered
over the thick

Bakelite phones for those
few seconds bleeding the last of love

out, when I think
to say their names,

together, I think

that disregard is
the final loneliness

the most female.

BUTOH

A form of Japanese dance . . . . that includes grotesque imagery, taboo topics,
extreme and controlled movements . . . .

The old dancer chews the dandelion greens
she stoops to pick from the field behind the school. The green

leaf is not smoky enough, is bitter tough, but the sun
shines off the black snakes in the low grass, makes a prism

indigo to red, reminds her of menstrual-blood art, and inspires
choreography: a plié crawl, a broken waltz, a butoh. *Look at the dyke*

pulling weeds for her lunch! a cruel boy cries from the chain
link shadows. But she has *chicoria* warm in her white apron's pouch

and black bread oily with salted
anchovies. Her hair grows static in the cold dry afternoon,

electric like Santa Lucia's crown. She'll stroke it down
smooth with her bone comb, her own spit and palm.

FATAL MOUTHS

The city guys are stringing Christmas lights on the locust trees.

The men are lifted in buckets. First, any old witches come down.

And then the forgotten paper pumpkins. The bats.

The city guys shake loose the dried locust pods: brown and curled

they land on Essex Street like snakes. Finally, the white

lights can go up and stay past the New Year.

If there is a God, His indifference has settled deep within

my ribcaged country. Last night, on television, I saw a woman scrubbed

of makeup give a speech. I read about a woman who screamed

but no one came. All over her body: fatal mouths

widened with a knife. The city guys string

white lights on bare branches, and wind them around

fat trunks tight and soon, all of Salem will glow.

I OFFER KITTY GENOVESE FAKE FRUIT

The gilt pears shine

like hooded eyelids

of the Madonna peering from the wall

in shame and piety. The black glass grapes

tight with silk and wire grow round

as your lover's eyes when she'd see you come

back into the room. Would she remember

your softness, Kitty? Like these velvet apples stuck

with pins and green

sequin-cloves? The fruit bleed

something dead and dusty in the lead

crystal bowl in my mother's parlor

in the old house where the lights

don't work, the gold cherub-sconces

unplugged from the walls. Outside,

the moon is new, unlit. *Eat.*

Stay here with me. Don't ever leave.

NOTES

"Men Who Are Afraid of Bats"—Sophia Farrar was the only person who came to Kitty's aid. She tried to comfort Kitty, who was still alive after the attack. Sophia held Kitty as they waited for the ambulance.

"Panis, Panis, Angelicus"—sources: Grace DiSanto, Elaine Romaine, Anne Paolucci, Kathy Freeperson, Phyllis Capello, Diane di Prima, Elizabeth Marraffino, Daniela Gioseffi, Maria Iannacome Coles, Anna Bart, Sandra M. Gilbert, Maria Mazziotti Gillan, Jacquelyn Bonomo, Theresa Vinciguerra

"Kim Jong-un's Half Brother was Murdered by Two Women with Poison Needles"— Kim Jong-nam was murdered in Malaysia on February 13, 2017. The nerve gas was at first thought to have been administered by needles.

"Kitty Genovese is Offered a Rorschach Print Dress"—Walter Kovacs (Rorschach) in the comic series, *The Watchmen*, wears a mask fashioned from a dress made for Kitty Genovese (which she never picked up from the tailor).

"38 Witnessed Her Death, I Witnessed her Love: The Lonely Secret of Mary Ann Zielonko"—LuLu LoLo wrote and performed this amazing play, recounting the relationship of Kitty Genovese and Mary Ann Zielonko

"From *Kitty Genovese: The Murder, the Bystanders, the Crime that Changed America*"—Kevin Cook, W.W. Norton and Co., March, 2014.

"Things Kitty Genovese Should Have"—*Ces bottes sont faites pour marcher (These boots are made for walking).*

ACKNOWLEDGMENTS

"Discussing Elephant Puppets the Night of the Refugee Ban"—*Apogee Journal*

"Necropoli"—*Arcturus* (*Chicago Review of Books*)

"At the Border"—*Bop Dead City*

"Equinox"—*Calamus Journal*

"Anniversary,"—*Carve Magazine*

"Fatal Mouths"—*Cleaver Magazine*

"Gold Bug Bagatelle," "Pomona Street"—*FRiGG*

"The Grape Arbor"—*Italian Americana*

"The Passion"—*MockingHeart Review*

"Men Who Are Afraid of Bats" "At the Plaza de Santa Croce"—*Nixes Mate Review*

"Colonial Acres," "Trump Tweets About Bloody Women," "Panis, Panis, Angelicus," "Cervical/Turn"—*Ovunque Siamo*

"Windows"—*petrichor*

"Astronomers Added the Unicorn to the Orion Constellation Family for Completeness," "In the North End," "Stencil of Kitty Genovese"—*Pithead Chapel*

"Tin Colander With Stars"—*Plath Poetry Project*

"The Lavender Menace"—*Silkworm*

"Crooked Forest"—*Sugar House Review*

"Kitty Genovese Names Her Fourteen Wounds"—*Third Point Press*

"Things Kitty Genovese Should Have"—*Thrush Poetry Journal*

"Artichoke Heart," "The Major Arcana of the Kitty Genovese Tarot,"
     "A God Lives in the Amygdala," "Kim-Jong Un's Half Brother
     Was Killed by Two Women With Needles," "I Offer Kitty
     Genovese Fake Fruit"—*Tinderbox Poetry Journal*

"Butoh"—*Vector Press*
     "Butoh" also appeared in *Nasty Women Poets : An Unapologetic
     Anthology of Subversive Verse*, edited by Grace Bauer and Julie
     Kane

"In the Light of the Hanging Globe Lamp," "Once Loosed," "After
     Bird," "Dear Kitty," "from *Kitty Genovese: The Murder, the
     Bystanders, the Crime that Changed America*," "Magical Thinking
     in the Time of Lyndon Johnson," "My Mother's Ashtrays," and
     "Genovese Basil at the Equinox," all appeared in the chapbook,
     After Bird, from Grey Book Press.

I conflated aspects Kitty Genovese's story as an Italian-American woman with my own, wove some of my own memories with her story. I don't know that Kitty typed on an Olivetti sitting at a Bauhaus desk; those iconic pieces were in my home, so I gave them to her; she gave me richness. Kitty continues to inform literature and pop culture: her story is that of a strong, modern, and much-loved woman living at a time of upheaval. I wonder what Kitty would think of our world now! I was blessed with incredible books that taught me so much about Kitty's personality and life, and how deeply she affected the people who loved her. The following were indispensable in my writing *My Tarantella*:

The Witness, Kitty Genovese: The Murder, the Bystanders, the Crime that Changed America, Kevin Cook; *Kitty Genovese: A True Account of a Public Murder and Its Private Consequences,* Catherine Pelonero; *No One Helped,* Marcia M. Gallo.

The documentary, *The Witness* (written by William Genovese, Russell Greene, Gabriel Rhodes, and James D. Solomon), which not only broke my heart, but began my journey with Kitty Genovese.

LuLu LoLo, for her brilliant performance: *38 Witnessed Her Death, I Witnessed Her Love: The Lonely Secret of Mary Ann Zielonko (Kitty Genovese Story).*

The Italian American Writers' Association and I AM Books in Boston's North End who let me read Kitty poem after Kitty poem, and for giving us a place to be.

Grey Book Press for seeing these Kitty Genovese poems as a whole.

Laurette Viteritti-Folk and Olivia Kate Cerrone, for the support and the sisterhood.

Jennifer Jean who found Kitty stenciled on a wall and who guided me with so many of these poems.

January Gill O'Neil, Cindy Veach, Carla Panciera, Danielle Jones, Rebecca Kinzie Bastian, Kali Lightfoot, Dawn Paul, Colleen Michaels,

M.P. Carver, Clay Ventre, Jim DiFillippi, J.D. Scrimgeour, Kevin Carey, Michelle Messina Reale—who lived with Kitty and my obsession.

Vin, Mia, and Michael Martelli.

Hillary Clinton, because I heard you.

ABOUT THE AUTHOR

Jennifer Martelli is the author of *The Uncanny Valley* (Big Table Publishing Company) as well as the chapbook, *After Bird* from Grey Book press. Her work has appeared in *The Aeolian Harp Anthology, The Superstition Review, The Bitter Oleander, Thrush, Carve, Glass Poetry Journal, The Heavy Feather Review*, and *Tinderbox Poetry Journal*. Jennifer Martelli is the recipient of the Massachusetts Cultural Council Grant in Poetry. She is a poetry editor at *The Mom Egg Review*.

VIA Folios

A refereed book series dedicated to the culture of Italians and Italian Americans.

MARIA TERRONE. *At Home in the New World.* Vol. 132. Essays. $16
GIL FAGIANI. *Missing Madonnas.* Vol. 131. Poetry. $14
LEWIS TURCO. *The Sonnetarium.* Vol. 130. Poetry. $12
JOE AMATO. *Samuel Taylor's Hollywood Adventure.* Vol. 129. Novel. $20
BEA TUSIANI. *Con Amore.* Vol. 128. Memoir. $16
MARIA GIURA. *What My Father Taught Me.* Vol. 127. Poetry. $12
STANISLAO PUGLIESE. *A Century of Sinatra.* Vol. 126. Popular Culture. $12
TONY ARDIZZONE. *The Arab's Ox.* Vol. 125. Novel. $18
PHYLLIS CAPELLO. *Packs Small Plays Big.* Vol. 124. Literature.
FRED GARDAPHÉ. *Read 'em and Reap.* Vol. 123. Criticism. $22
JOSEPH A. AMATO. *Diagnostics.* Vol 122. Literature. $12.
DENNIS BARONE. *Second Thoughts.* Vol 121. Poetry. $10
OLIVIA K. CERRONE. *The Hunger Saint.* Vol 120. Novella. $12
GARIBLADI M. LAPOLLA. *Miss Rollins in Love.* Vol 119. Novel. $24
JOSEPH TUSIANI. *A Clarion Call.* Vol 118. Poetry. $16
JOSEPH A. AMATO. *My Three Sicilies.* Vol 117. Poetry & Prose. $17
MARGHERITA COSTA. *Voice of a Virtuosa and Coutesan.* Vol 116. Poetry. $24
NICOLE SANTALUCIA. *Because I Did Not Die.* Vol 115. Poetry. $12
MARK CIABATTARI. *Preludes to History.* Vol 114. Poetry. $12
HELEN BAROLINI. *Visits.* Vol 113. Novel. $22
ERNESTO LIVORNI. *The Fathers' America.* Vol 112. Poetry. $14
MARIO B. MIGNONE. *The Story of My People.* Vol 111. Non-fiction. $17
GEORGE GUIDA. *The Sleeping Gulf.* Vol 110. Poetry. $14
JOEY NICOLETTI. *Reverse Graffiti.* Vol 109. Poetry. $14
GIOSE RIMANELLI. *Il mestiere del furbo.* Vol 108. Criticism. $20
LEWIS TURCO. *The Hero Enkidu.* Vol 107. Poetry. $14
AL TACCONELLI. *Perhaps Fly.* Vol 106. Poetry. $14
RACHEL GUIDO DEVRIES. *A Woman Unknown in Her Bones.* Vol 105.
    Poetry. $11
BERNARD BRUNO. *A Tear and a Tear in My Heart.* Vol 104. Non-fiction. $20
FELIX STEFANILE. *Songs of the Sparrow.* Vol 103. Poetry. $30
FRANK POLIZZI. *A New Life with Bianca.* Vol 102. Poetry. $10
GIL FAGIANI. *Stone Walls.* Vol 101. Poetry. $14
LOUISE DESALVO. *Casting Off.* Vol 100. Fiction. $22
MARY JO BONA. *I Stop Waiting for You.* Vol 99. Poetry. $12
RACHEL GUIDO DEVRIES. *Stati zitt, Josie.* Vol 98. Children's Literature. $8
GRACE CAVALIERI. *The Mandate of Heaven.* Vol 97. Poetry. $14
MARISA FRASCA. *Via incanto.* Vol 96. Poetry. $12
DOUGLAS GLADSTONE. *Carving a Niche for Himself.* Vol 95. History. $12
MARIA TERRONE. *Eye to Eye.* Vol 94. Poetry. $14
CONSTANCE SANCETTA. *Here in Cerchio.* Vol 93. Local History. $15

MARIA MAZZIOTTI GILLAN. *Ancestors' Song*. Vol 92. Poetry. $14

MICHAEL PARENTI. *Waiting for Yesterday: Pages from a Street Kid's Life*. Vol 90. Memoir. $15

ANNIE LANZILLOTTO. *Schistsong*. Vol 89. Poetry. $15

EMANUEL DI PASQUALE. *Love Lines*. Vol 88. Poetry. $10

CAROSONE & LOGIUDICE. *Our Naked Lives*. Vol 87. Essays. $15

JAMES PERICONI. *Strangers in a Strange Land: A Survey of Italian-Language American Books*.Vol 86. Book History. $24

DANIELA GIOSEFFI. *Escaping La Vita Della Cucina*. Vol 85. Essays. $22

MARIA FAMÀ. *Mystics in the Family*. Vol 84. Poetry. $10

ROSSANA DEL ZIO. *From Bread and Tomatoes to Zuppa di Pesce "Ciambotto"*.Vol. 83. $15

LORENZO DELBOCA. *Polentoni*. Vol 82. Italian Studies. $15

SAMUEL GHELLI. *A Reference Grammar*. Vol 81. Italian Language. $36

ROSS TALARICO. *Sled Run*. Vol 80. Fiction. $15

FRED MISURELLA. *Only Sons*. Vol 79. Fiction. $14

FRANK LENTRICCHIA. *The Portable Lentricchia*. Vol 78. Fiction. $16

RICHARD VETERE. *The Other Colors in a Snow Storm*. Vol 77. Poetry. $10

GARIBALDI LAPOLLA. *Fire in the Flesh*. Vol 76 Fiction & Criticism. $25

GEORGE GUIDA. *The Pope Stories*. Vol 75 Prose. $15

ROBERT VISCUSI. *Ellis Island*. Vol 74. Poetry. $28

ELENA GIANINI BELOTTI. *The Bitter Taste of Strangers Bread*. Vol 73. Fiction. $24

PINO APRILE. *Terroni*. Vol 72. Italian Studies. $20

EMANUEL DI PASQUALE. *Harvest*. Vol 71. Poetry. $10

ROBERT ZWEIG. *Return to Naples*. Vol 70. Memoir. $16

AIROS & CAPPELLI. *Guido*. Vol 69. Italian/American Studies. $12

FRED GARDAPHÉ. *Moustache Pete is Dead! Long Live Moustache Pete!*. Vol 67. Literature/Oral History. $12

PAOLO RUFFILLI. *Dark Room/Camera oscura*. Vol 66. Poetry. $11

HELEN BAROLINI. *Crossing the Alps*. Vol 65. Fiction. $14

COSMO FERRARA. *Profiles of Italian Americans*. Vol 64. Italian Americana. $16

GIL FAGIANI. *Chianti in Connecticut*. Vol 63. Poetry. $10

BASSETTI & D'ACQUINO. *Italic Lessons*. Vol 62. Italian/American Studies. $10

CAVALIERI & PASCARELLI, Eds. *The Poet's Cookbook*. Vol 61. Poetry/Recipes. $12

EMANUEL DI PASQUALE. *Siciliana*. Vol 60. Poetry. $8

NATALIA COSTA, Ed. *Bufalini*. Vol 59. Poetry. $18.

RICHARD VETERE. *Baroque*. Vol 58. Fiction. $18.

LEWIS TURCO. *La Famiglia/The Family*. Vol 57. Memoir. $15

NICK JAMES MILETI. *The Unscrupulous*. Vol 56. Humanities. $20

BASSETTI. ACCOLLA. D'AQUINO. *Italici: An Encounter with Piero Bassetti*. Vol 55. Italian Studies. $8

GIOSE RIMANELLI. *The Three-legged One*. Vol 54. Fiction. $15

CHARLES KLOPP. *Bele Antiche Stòrie*. Vol 53. Criticism. $25

JOSEPH RICAPITO. *Second Wave*. Vol 52. Poetry. $12

GARY MORMINO. *Italians in Florida*. Vol 51. History. $15

GIANFRANCO ANGELUCCI. *Federico F*. Vol 50. Fiction. $15

ANTHONY VALERIO. *The Little Sailor*. Vol 49. Memoir. $9

ROSS TALARICO. *The Reptilian Interludes*. Vol 48. Poetry. $15

RACHEL GUIDO DE VRIES. *Teeny Tiny Tino's Fishing Story*. Vol 47. Children's Literature. $6

EMANUEL DI PASQUALE. *Writing Anew*. Vol 46. Poetry. $15

MARIA FAMÀ. *Looking For Cover*. Vol 45. Poetry. $12

ANTHONY VALERIO. *Toni Cade Bambara's One Sicilian Night*. Vol 44. Poetry. $10

EMANUEL CARNEVALI. *Furnished Rooms*. Vol 43. Poetry. $14

BRENT ADKINS. et al., Ed. *Shifting Borders. Negotiating Places*. Vol 42. Conference. $18

GEORGE GUIDA. *Low Italian*. Vol 41. Poetry. $11

GARDAPHÈ, GIORDANO, TAMBURRI. *Introducing Italian Americana*. Vol 40. Italian/American Studies. $10

DANIELA GIOSEFFI. *Blood Autumn/Autunno di sangue*. Vol 39. Poetry. $15/$25

FRED MISURELLA. *Lies to Live By*. Vol 38. Stories. $15

STEVEN BELLUSCIO. *Constructing a Bibliography*. Vol 37. Italian Americana. $15

ANTHONY JULIAN TAMBURRI, Ed. *Italian Cultural Studies 2002*. Vol 36. Essays. $18

BEA TUSIANI. *con amore*. Vol 35. Memoir. $19

FLAVIA BRIZIO-SKOV, Ed. *Reconstructing Societies in the Aftermath of War*. Vol 34. History. $30

TAMBURRI. et al., Eds. *Italian Cultural Studies 2001*. Vol 33. Essays. $18

ELIZABETH G. MESSINA, Ed. *In Our Own Voices*. Vol 32. Italian/American Studies. $25

STANISLAO G. PUGLIESE. *Desperate Inscriptions*. Vol 31. History. $12

HOSTERT & TAMBURRI, Eds. *Screening Ethnicity*. Vol 30. Italian/American Culture. $25

G. PARATI & B. LAWTON, Eds. *Italian Cultural Studies*. Vol 29. Essays. $18

HELEN BAROLINI. *More Italian Hours*. Vol 28. Fiction. $16

FRANCO NASI, Ed. *Intorno alla Via Emilia*. Vol 27. Culture. $16

ARTHUR L. CLEMENTS. *The Book of Madness & Love*. Vol 26. Poetry. $10

JOHN CASEY, et al. *Imagining Humanity*. Vol 25. Interdisciplinary Studies. $18

ROBERT LIMA. *Sardinia/Sardegna*. Vol 24. Poetry. $10

DANIELA GIOSEFFI. *Going On*. Vol 23. Poetry. $10

ROSS TALARICO. *The Journey Home*. Vol 22. Poetry. $12

EMANUEL DI PASQUALE. *The Silver Lake Love Poems*. Vol 21. Poetry. $7

JOSEPH TUSIANI. *Ethnicity*. Vol 20. Poetry. $12

JENNIFER LAGIER. *Second Class Citizen*. Vol 19. Poetry. $8

FELIX STEFANILE. *The Country of Absence*. Vol 18. Poetry. $9

PHILIP CANNISTRARO. *Blackshirts*. Vol 17. History. $12

LUIGI RUSTICHELLI, Ed. *Seminario sul racconto*. Vol 16. Narrative. $10

LEWIS TURCO. *Shaking the Family Tree*. Vol 15. Memoirs. $9

LUIGI RUSTICHELLI, Ed. *Seminario sulla drammaturgia*. Vol 14. Theater/ Essays. $10

FRED GARDAPHÈ. *Moustache Pete is Dead! Long Live Moustache Pete!*. Vol 13. Oral Literature. $10

JONE GAILLARD CORSI. *Il libretto d'autore. 1860 – 1930*. Vol 12. Criticism. $17

HELEN BAROLINI. *Chiaroscuro: Essays of Identity*. Vol 11. Essays. $15

PICARAZZI & FEINSTEIN, Eds. *An African Harlequin in Milan*. Vol 10. Theater/Essays. $15

JOSEPH RICAPITO. *Florentine Streets & Other Poems*. Vol 9. Poetry. $9

FRED MISURELLA. *Short Time*. Vol 8. Novella. $7

NED CONDINI. *Quartettsatz*. Vol 7. Poetry. $7

ANTHONY JULIAN TAMBURRI, Ed. *Fuori: Essays by Italian/American Lesbiansand Gays*. Vol 6. Essays. $10

ANTONIO GRAMSCI. P. Verdicchio. Trans. & Intro. *The Southern Question*. Vol 5.Social Criticism. $5

DANIELA GIOSEFFI. *Word Wounds & Water Flowers*. Vol 4. Poetry. $8

WILEY FEINSTEIN. *Humility's Deceit: Calvino Reading Ariosto Reading Calvino*. Vol 3. Criticism. $10

PAOLO A. GIORDANO, Ed. *Joseph Tusiani: Poet. Translator. Humanist*. Vol 2. Criticism. $25

ROBERT VISCUSI. *Oration Upon the Most Recent Death of Christopher Columbus*. Vol 1. Poetry.

CPSIA information can be obtained
at www.ICGtesting.com
Printed in the USA
FFHW02n1703041018
48684792-52705FF

9 781599 541303